A Great Day

With a positive attitude, I will have a great day!

Oh no! My shoelace broke.

Oh well. I can solve this problem.
I will fix my shoelace.

Oops! I spilled my milk.

That's OK. I can solve this problem.
I will clean it up.

Oh no! I ripped my folder.

This is easy. I can solve this problem.
I will fix it with tape.

Oh no! My favorite seat on the bus is taken.

That's OK. I can solve this problem.
I will find another seat.

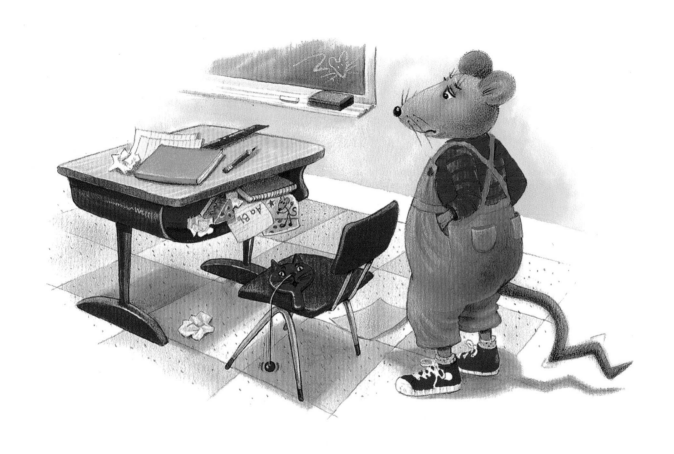

Look at this! My desk is very messy.

This is easy. I can solve this problem.
I will make it neat.

Oh no! My friend is sick at home.

I know what to do.
I will play with another friend.

Today I had many problems.
Sometimes it's hard to have a great day.

But I *did* have a great day.
Do you know why?

I had a great day because I had a positive attitude.
And I solved my problems one by one!